FRIENDS LISTOGRAPHY

OUR LIVES IN LISTS

Created by Lisa Nola
Illustrations by Maria Forde

CHRONICLE BOOKS
SAN FRANCISCO

This book is dedicated to my friends and family,
and to Adam, who has been an endless source of
friendship, love, and support.

Text copyright © 2010 by Lisa Nola.
Illustrations copyright © 2010 by Maria Forde.

ISBN: 978-0-8118-6975-1

Manufactured in China.

Design by Kristen Hewitt.
Illustrations by Maria Forde.
Hand lettering by Claire Fletcher.

10 9 8 7 6 5 4 3

Chronicle Books LLC
680 Second Street
San Francisco, CA 94107

www.chroniclebooks.com

INTRODUCTION

FRIENDS LISTOGRAPHY IS A GREAT WAY TO ENTERTAIN
YOUR GUESTS AT A DINNER PARTY, GET TO KNOW YOUR
FRIENDS AT SCHOOL MORE INTIMATELY, OR DISCOVER
LITTLE DETAILS ABOUT YOUR COWORKERS. FILL IT IN
COLLECTIVELY AND READ WHAT COMES BACK. CONSIDER
THIS A FRIENDLY SLAM BOOK IN LIST FORM.
I HOPE IT BRINGS LOTS OF FUN!

LISA NOLA

VISIT US AT WWW.LISTOGRAPHY.COM

LISTOGRAPHY FRIENDS SIGN IN HERE:

INITIAL
HERE

- ☐

- ☐

- ☐

- ☐

- ☐

- ☐

- ☐

- ☐

- ☐

- ☐

- ☐

- ☐

- ☐

- ☐

- ☐

- ☐

- ☐

- ☐

May 19, 1978
Jr. Sr. Prom

HEATHER AND AARON

LIST WHICH FRIENDS WOULD WIN
PROM QUEEN & PROM KING

PROM QUEEN	PROM KING	INITIAL HERE
------------------------------	------------------------------	☐
------------------------------	------------------------------	☐
------------------------------	------------------------------	☐
------------------------------	------------------------------	☐
------------------------------	------------------------------	☐
------------------------------	------------------------------	☐
------------------------------	------------------------------	☐
------------------------------	------------------------------	☐
------------------------------	------------------------------	☐
------------------------------	------------------------------	☐
------------------------------	------------------------------	☐
------------------------------	------------------------------	☐
------------------------------	------------------------------	☐
------------------------------	------------------------------	☐
------------------------------	------------------------------	☐
------------------------------	------------------------------	☐
------------------------------	------------------------------	☐
------------------------------	------------------------------	☐
------------------------------	------------------------------	☐

DAN: THE IRON CHEF

LIST SOME POSSIBLE NEW NICKNAMES
FOR FRIENDS

FRIEND	NICKNAME	INITIAL HERE
		☐
		☐
		☐
		☐
		☐
		☐
		☐
		☐
		☐
		☐
		☐
		☐
		☐
		☐
		☐
		☐
		☐
		☐
		☐

MARC'S UNICORN COLLECTION—
DRESSER, BOTTOM DRAWER

LIST WHOSE HOUSES YOU'D PILLAGE FOR TREASURE AND WHAT YOU'D TAKE

FRIEND	TREASURE	INITIAL HERE
		☐
		☐
		☐
		☐
		☐
		☐
		☐
		☐
		☐
		☐
		☐
		☐
		☐
		☐
		☐
		☐
		☐
		☐
		☐
		☐

PROBABLY NOT ME

LIST WHICH FRIENDS WIN THE BEST-DRESSED AWARDS

INITIAL HERE

-------------------------------- [ ]
-------------------------------- [ ]
-------------------------------- [ ]
-------------------------------- [ ]
-------------------------------- [ ]
-------------------------------- [ ]
-------------------------------- [ ]
-------------------------------- [ ]
-------------------------------- [ ]
-------------------------------- [ ]
-------------------------------- [ ]
-------------------------------- [ ]
-------------------------------- [ ]
-------------------------------- [ ]
-------------------------------- [ ]
-------------------------------- [ ]
-------------------------------- [ ]
-------------------------------- [ ]
-------------------------------- [ ]

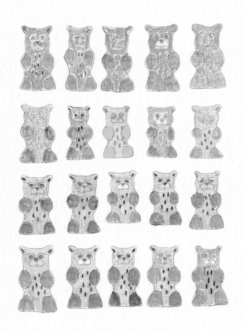

NO YELLOW GUMMI BEARS!!

LIST WHO HAS EARNED THE MOST DIVA AND DRAMA QUEEN POINTS

INITIAL
HERE

------------------------------ ☐

------------------------------ ☐

------------------------------ ☐

------------------------------ ☐

------------------------------ ☐

------------------------------ ☐

------------------------------ ☐

------------------------------ ☐

------------------------------ ☐

------------------------------ ☐

------------------------------ ☐

------------------------------ ☐

------------------------------ ☐

------------------------------ ☐

------------------------------ ☐

------------------------------ ☐

------------------------------ ☐

------------------------------ ☐

------------------------------ ☐

------------------------------ ☐

SCOTT BECAUSE HE VOLUNTEERS ON THE WEEKENDS

LIST WHO HAS EARNED THE MOST GIRL SCOUT OR BOY SCOUT BADGES

FRIEND	BECAUSE	INITIAL HERE
		☐
		☐
		☐
		☐
		☐
		☐
		☐
		☐
		☐
		☐
		☐
		☐
		☐
		☐
		☐
		☐
		☐
		☐
		☐
		☐

BEYONCÉ = SASHA FIERCE

LIST WHO HAS A SPLIT PERSONALITY
OR AN ALTER EGO

INITIAL HERE

----------- = -----------
----------- = -----------
----------- = -----------
----------- = -----------
----------- = -----------
----------- = -----------
----------- = -----------
----------- = -----------
----------- = -----------
----------- = -----------
----------- = -----------
----------- = -----------
----------- = -----------
----------- = -----------
----------- = -----------
----------- = -----------
----------- = -----------
----------- = -----------
----------- = -----------
----------- = -----------

DUANE + LION = DION

LIST WHO REMINDS YOU OF CERTAIN ANIMALS

FRIEND   ANIMAL   INITIAL
                                                    HERE

GET READY TO RUMBLE

LIST FRIENDS WHO WOULD MAKE A GOOD MATCHUP IN THE RING (CIRCLE WHO YOU'D BET ON)

INITIAL
HERE

---------------------------- VS. ---------------------------- ☐

---------------------------- VS. ---------------------------- ☐

---------------------------- VS. ---------------------------- ☐

---------------------------- VS. ---------------------------- ☐

---------------------------- VS. ---------------------------- ☐

---------------------------- VS. ---------------------------- ☐

---------------------------- VS. ---------------------------- ☐

---------------------------- VS. ---------------------------- ☐

---------------------------- VS. ---------------------------- ☐

---------------------------- VS. ---------------------------- ☐

---------------------------- VS. ---------------------------- ☐

---------------------------- VS. ---------------------------- ☐

---------------------------- VS. ---------------------------- ☐

---------------------------- VS. ---------------------------- ☐

---------------------------- VS. ---------------------------- ☐

---------------------------- VS. ---------------------------- ☐

---------------------------- VS. ---------------------------- ☐

---------------------------- VS. ---------------------------- ☐

---------------------------- VS. ---------------------------- ☐

SALMA'S CONFIDENCE

LIST WHOSE CHARACTER TRAITS YOU ADMIRE

FRIEND	TRAIT	INITIAL HERE
		☐
		☐
		☐
		☐
		☐
		☐
		☐
		☐
		☐
		☐
		☐
		☐
		☐
		☐
		☐
		☐
		☐
		☐
		☐

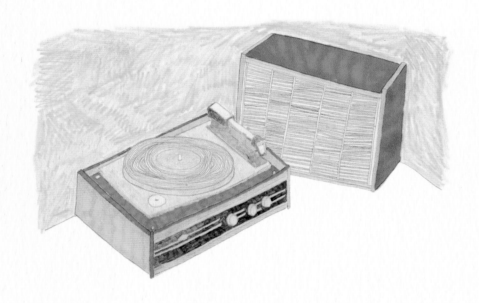

SONYA = NIGHT RANGER'S
"SISTER CHRISTIAN"

LIST A SONG THAT CAPTURES A FRIEND PERFECTLY

FRIEND		SONG	INITIAL HERE
-------------------------	=	-------------------------	☐
-------------------------	=	-------------------------	☐
-------------------------	=	-------------------------	☐
-------------------------	=	-------------------------	☐
-------------------------	=	-------------------------	☐
-------------------------	=	-------------------------	☐
-------------------------	=	-------------------------	☐
-------------------------	=	-------------------------	☐
-------------------------	=	-------------------------	☐
-------------------------	=	-------------------------	☐
-------------------------	=	-------------------------	☐
-------------------------	=	-------------------------	☐
-------------------------	=	-------------------------	☐
-------------------------	=	-------------------------	☐
-------------------------	=	-------------------------	☐
-------------------------	=	-------------------------	☐
-------------------------	=	-------------------------	☐
-------------------------	=	-------------------------	☐
-------------------------	=	-------------------------	☐

THE DAILYSHOW

RICHARD REMINDS ME OF THAT GUY ON TV

LIST WHO COMES THE CLOSEST TO HAVING
A CELEBRITY LOOK-ALIKE

FRIEND	CELEB-U-LIKE	INITIAL HERE
		☐
		☐
		☐
		☐
		☐
		☐
		☐
		☐
		☐
		☐
		☐
		☐
		☐
		☐
		☐
		☐
		☐
		☐
		☐

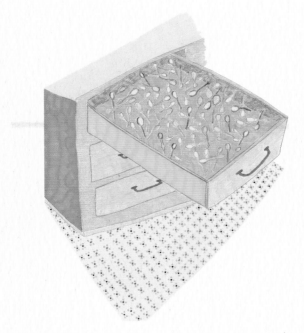

LIANE BORROWS SPOONS FROM RESTAURANTS

LIST WHAT SINS OR CRIMES YOU'VE WITNESSED FRIENDS COMMITTING

FRIEND	GUILTY OF	INITIAL HERE

CYNTHIA WILL MAKE ME A CUPCAKE
ON THE 1st OF EVERY MONTH

LIST WHICH SPELL YOU'D CAST ON A FRIEND

FRIEND	SPELL	INITIAL HERE
		☐
		☐
		☐
		☐
		☐
		☐
		☐
		☐
		☐
		☐
		☐
		☐
		☐
		☐
		☐
		☐
		☐
		☐
		☐
		☐

ADRIENNE AND TWO YEARS OF PRACTICE

LIST WHO'S GOT TALENT

FRIEND   TALENT   INITIAL
                                                                            HERE

------------------------------------   ------------------------------------   ☐
------------------------------------   ------------------------------------   ☐
------------------------------------   ------------------------------------   ☐
------------------------------------   ------------------------------------   ☐
------------------------------------   ------------------------------------   ☐
------------------------------------   ------------------------------------   ☐
------------------------------------   ------------------------------------   ☐
------------------------------------   ------------------------------------   ☐
------------------------------------   ------------------------------------   ☐
------------------------------------   ------------------------------------   ☐
------------------------------------   ------------------------------------   ☐
------------------------------------   ------------------------------------   ☐
------------------------------------   ------------------------------------   ☐
------------------------------------   ------------------------------------   ☐
------------------------------------   ------------------------------------   ☐
------------------------------------   ------------------------------------   ☐
------------------------------------   ------------------------------------   ☐
------------------------------------   ------------------------------------   ☐
------------------------------------   ------------------------------------   ☐

NO PROBLEM

LIST THREE FRIENDS/CONTENDERS YOU THINK YOU
COULD BEAT AT ARM WRESTLING

①   ②   ③   INITIAL
                                                      HERE

_____   _____   _____   ☐

_____   _____   _____   ☐

_____   _____   _____   ☐

_____   _____   _____   ☐

_____   _____   _____   ☐

_____   _____   _____   ☐

_____   _____   _____   ☐

_____   _____   _____   ☐

_____   _____   _____   ☐

_____   _____   _____   ☐

_____   _____   _____   ☐

_____   _____   _____   ☐

_____   _____   _____   ☐

_____   _____   _____   ☐

_____   _____   _____   ☐

_____   _____   _____   ☐

_____   _____   _____   ☐

_____   _____   _____   ☐

_____   _____   _____   ☐

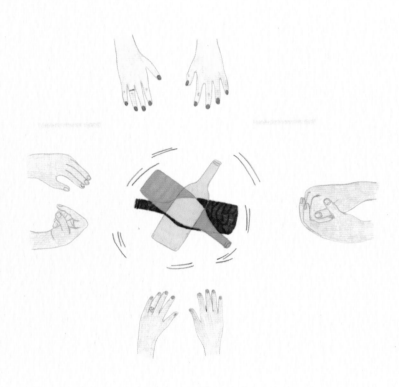

ONLY IF I HAD TO

LIST THREE FRIENDS YOU'D KISS IF YOU HAD TO

①   ②   ③   INITIAL HERE

MacGYVER

MATT IS MACGYVER

LIST WHICH FILM OR TV CHARACTER ROLES YOUR FRIENDS COULD SLIP INTO SEAMLESSLY

FRIEND	ROLE	INITIAL HERE

ANDREA'S CURLY HAIR
ON HUMID DAYS

LIST WHOSE PHYSICAL FEATURES
YOU ADMIRE

FRIEND   FEATURE   INITIAL
                                                                            HERE

--------------------------   --------------------------   ☐

--------------------------   --------------------------   ☐

--------------------------   --------------------------   ☐

--------------------------   --------------------------   ☐

--------------------------   --------------------------   ☐

--------------------------   --------------------------   ☐

--------------------------   --------------------------   ☐

--------------------------   --------------------------   ☐

--------------------------   --------------------------   ☐

--------------------------   --------------------------   ☐

--------------------------   --------------------------   ☐

--------------------------   --------------------------   ☐

--------------------------   --------------------------   ☐

--------------------------   --------------------------   ☐

--------------------------   --------------------------   ☐

--------------------------   --------------------------   ☐

--------------------------   --------------------------   ☐

--------------------------   --------------------------   ☐

--------------------------   --------------------------   ☐

JUSTIN WATCHED EVERY EPISODE OF "LOST"

LIST WHICH FRIENDS YOU'D TAKE IF YOU WERE STRANDED ON A DESERTED ISLAND AND WHY

FRIEND WHY INITIAL HERE

-----------------------------   -----------------------------   ☐
-----------------------------   -----------------------------   ☐
-----------------------------   -----------------------------   ☐
-----------------------------   -----------------------------   ☐
-----------------------------   -----------------------------   ☐
-----------------------------   -----------------------------   ☐
-----------------------------   -----------------------------   ☐
-----------------------------   -----------------------------   ☐
-----------------------------   -----------------------------   ☐
-----------------------------   -----------------------------   ☐
-----------------------------   -----------------------------   ☐
-----------------------------   -----------------------------   ☐
-----------------------------   -----------------------------   ☐
-----------------------------   -----------------------------   ☐
-----------------------------   -----------------------------   ☐
-----------------------------   -----------------------------   ☐
-----------------------------   -----------------------------   ☐
-----------------------------   -----------------------------   ☐
-----------------------------   -----------------------------   ☐

Personalize
Your
Lifestyle!

LAURA HAS A TENDENCY TO REDECORATE
EVERYDAY OBJECTS

LIST WHO HAS WEIRD HABITS

FRIEND	WEIRDNESS	INITIAL HERE
- - - - - - - - - - - - - - - -	- - - - - - - - - - - - - - - -	☐
- - - - - - - - - - - - - - - -	- - - - - - - - - - - - - - - -	☐
- - - - - - - - - - - - - - - -	- - - - - - - - - - - - - - - -	☐
- - - - - - - - - - - - - - - -	- - - - - - - - - - - - - - - -	☐
- - - - - - - - - - - - - - - -	- - - - - - - - - - - - - - - -	☐
- - - - - - - - - - - - - - - -	- - - - - - - - - - - - - - - -	☐
- - - - - - - - - - - - - - - -	- - - - - - - - - - - - - - - -	☐
- - - - - - - - - - - - - - - -	- - - - - - - - - - - - - - - -	☐
- - - - - - - - - - - - - - - -	- - - - - - - - - - - - - - - -	☐
- - - - - - - - - - - - - - - -	- - - - - - - - - - - - - - - -	☐
- - - - - - - - - - - - - - - -	- - - - - - - - - - - - - - - -	☐
- - - - - - - - - - - - - - - -	- - - - - - - - - - - - - - - -	☐
- - - - - - - - - - - - - - - -	- - - - - - - - - - - - - - - -	☐
- - - - - - - - - - - - - - - -	- - - - - - - - - - - - - - - -	☐
- - - - - - - - - - - - - - - -	- - - - - - - - - - - - - - - -	☐
- - - - - - - - - - - - - - - -	- - - - - - - - - - - - - - - -	☐
- - - - - - - - - - - - - - - -	- - - - - - - - - - - - - - - -	☐
- - - - - - - - - - - - - - - -	- - - - - - - - - - - - - - - -	☐
- - - - - - - - - - - - - - - -	- - - - - - - - - - - - - - - -	☐

STEVE IS COUNTRY AND VINCE
IS ROCK AND ROLL

LIST WHO'S A LITTLE BIT COUNTRY AND WHO'S A LITTLE BIT ROCK AND ROLL

LITTLE BIT COUNTRY	LITTLE BIT ROCK + ROLL	INITIAL HERE
		☐
		☐
		☐
		☐
		☐
		☐
		☐
		☐
		☐
		☐
		☐
		☐
		☐
		☐
		☐
		☐
		☐
		☐
		☐

"YOU JUST BOUGHT YOURSELF ANOTHER SATURDAY."

LIST WHICH FRIENDS WOULD BE CAST AS ONE OF
THE CHARACTERS IN "THE BREAKFAST CLUB":
THE PRINCESS, THE CRIMINAL, THE BRAIN, THE ATHLETE,
OR THE BASKET CASE

FRIEND	CHARACTER	INITIAL HERE
		☐
		☐
		☐
		☐
		☐
		☐
		☐
		☐
		☐
		☐
		☐
		☐
		☐
		☐
		☐
		☐
		☐
		☐
		☐

ERIC IS TROUBLE

LIST WHO YOUR PARENTS WOULD TELL YOU TO STOP HANGING OUT WITH AND WHY

FRIEND   WHY   INITIAL
HERE

BEWARE!
HAUNTED
HOUSE
THIS WAY→

JOE FOR HOLDING MY HAND

LIST SOME THANK-YOU SHOUT-OUTS

FRIEND	SHOUT-OUT	INITIAL HERE
		☐
		☐
		☐
		☐
		☐
		☐
		☐
		☐
		☐
		☐
		☐
		☐
		☐
		☐
		☐
		☐
		☐
		☐
		☐
		☐

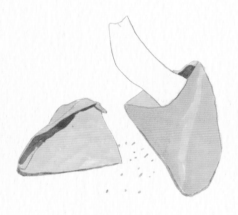

YOU WILL FIND A NEW LOVE IN YOUR FUTURE

LIST WHAT PREDICTIONS SOME FRIENDS MIGHT FIND
IN THEIR FORTUNE COOKIES

FRIEND	PREDICTION	INITIAL HERE
		☐
		☐
		☐
		☐
		☐
		☐
		☐
		☐
		☐
		☐
		☐
		☐
		☐
		☐
		☐
		☐
		☐
		☐
		☐
		☐

AUDRA AND CHRIS

LIST WHICH FRIENDS YOU'D THROW TOGETHER FOR A GUARANTEED HIT REALITY TV SHOW

①   ②   ③

INITIAL
HERE

HOMEMADE STUFFED ANIMALS

MIKE WOULD BE A GREAT TAXIDERMIST

LIST WHICH PROFESSIONS CERTAIN FRIENDS WOULD BE GREAT AT

FRIEND	JOB RECOMMENDATION	INITIAL HERE
		☐
		☐
		☐
		☐
		☐
		☐
		☐
		☐
		☐
		☐
		☐
		☐
		☐
		☐
		☐
		☐
		☐
		☐
		☐

I TAKE WOODSHOP CLASSES ON TUESDAY NIGHTS

LIST SOME FACTS PEOPLE PROBABLY DON'T KNOW ABOUT YOU

INITIAL
HERE

-- ☐

-- ☐

-- ☐

-- ☐

-- ☐

-- ☐

-- ☐

-- ☐

-- ☐

-- ☐

-- ☐

-- ☐

-- ☐

-- ☐

-- ☐

-- ☐

-- ☐

-- ☐

-- ☐

DIORAMAS OF PREHISTORIC FORESTS

LIST THREE GIFTS YOU WOULD LOVE TO RECEIVE

①   ②   ③   INITIAL HERE

A CURE FOR BREAST CANCER

LIST THREE WISHES FOR THE WORLD

①   ②   ③   INITIAL HERE

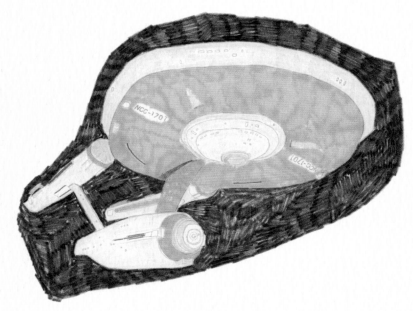

ALL THE "STAR TREKS"

LIST YOUR TOP THREE FAVORITE MOVIES

①   ②   ③   INITIAL HERE

THE JESUS AND MARY CHAIN

LIST YOUR TOP THREE FAVORITE BANDS

①   ②   ③   INITIAL HERE

WORKING WITH MONKEYS

LIST YOUR TOP THREE DREAM JOBS

①   ②   ③   INITIAL HERE

I EAT PIZZA FOR BREAKFAST

LIST AN EMBARRASSING CONFESSION

INITIAL
HERE

--- ☐
--- ☐
--- ☐
--- ☐
--- ☐
--- ☐
--- ☐
--- ☐
--- ☐
--- ☐
--- ☐
--- ☐
--- ☐
--- ☐
--- ☐
--- ☐
--- ☐
--- ☐

MARK WAHLBERG, THE "GOOD VIBRATIONS" YEARS

LIST YOUR TOP THREE CRUSHES

①   ②   ③   INITIAL HERE

I JUST WANT TO WEAR
THE COSTUMES

LIST THREE SUPERPOWERS YOU WISH YOU HAD

①   ②   ③   INITIAL
                                                    HERE

ham   green pepper   bacon   mushrooms   pepperoni   jalapeños   anchovies   pineapple   onion   olives

BUILD-YOUR-OWN PIZZA RESTAURANT

LIST YOUR BEST NEW BUSINESS OR INVENTION IDEAS

INITIAL
HERE

-- ☐

-- ☐

-- ☐

-- ☐

-- ☐

-- ☐

-- ☐

-- ☐

-- ☐

-- ☐

-- ☐

-- ☐

-- ☐

-- ☐

-- ☐

-- ☐

-- ☐

-- ☐

-- ☐

THE BROOKLYN BRIDGE IN THE SUMMERTIME

LIST THE THREE BEST PLACES FOR A DATE NIGHT IN YOUR TOWN

①   ②   ③   INITIAL HERE

THE TOWN UNICYCLISTS

LIST THE WEIRDEST THINGS YOU'VE WITNESSED IN PUBLIC

INITIAL
HERE

-- ☐

-- ☐

-- ☐

-- ☐

-- ☐

-- ☐

-- ☐

-- ☐

-- ☐

-- ☐

-- ☐

-- ☐

-- ☐

-- ☐

-- ☐

-- ☐

-- ☐

-- ☐

-- ☐

MOM AND DAD AS VAMPIRES

LIST SOME THINGS THAT ALWAYS APPEAR
IN YOUR DREAMS

INITIAL
HERE

- ☐
- ☐
- ☐
- ☐
- ☐
- ☐
- ☐
- ☐
- ☐
- ☐
- ☐
- ☐
- ☐
- ☐
- ☐
- ☐
- ☐
- ☐

MY BOARD GAME STASH

LIST YOUR BEST CHEERING UP RECIPES

INITIAL
HERE

THE RUSSIAN RIVER, NORTHERN CALIFORNIA

LIST YOUR TOP THREE VACATION DESTINATIONS

①   ②   ③   INITIAL HERE

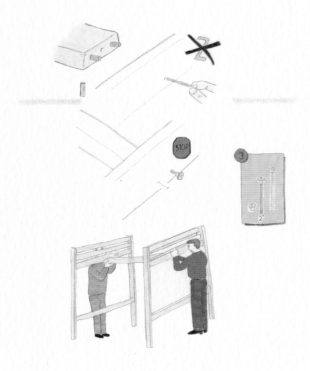

ASSEMBLING FURNITURE

LIST THREE THINGS YOU ARE
EXCEPTIONALLY GOOD AT

①   ②   ③

INITIAL
HERE

IF ONLY THEY GOT ALONG

LIST THREE FAVORITE THINGS YOU OWN

①   ②   ③   INITIAL HERE

5TH GRADE: LOST MY FRONT TOOTH
AFTER A TUMBLE

LIST YOUR MOST MEMORABLE INJURIES

INITIAL
HERE

- ☐

- ☐

- ☐

- ☐

- ☐

- ☐

- ☐

- ☐

- ☐

- ☐

- ☐

- ☐

- ☐

- ☐

- ☐

- ☐

- ☐

- ☐

- ☐

BUNGEE JUMP

LIST THINGS YOU'D NEVER EVER DO

INITIAL
HERE

- -

- -

- -

- -

- -

- -

- -

- -

- -

- -

- -

- -

- -

- -

- -

- -

- -

- -

- -

MY SEXY BIRTHMARK

LIST YOUR THREE MOST IDENTIFIABLE FEATURES

①   ②   ③   INITIAL HERE

BROKEN DISCARDED UMBRELLAS IN THE STREET

LIST THINGS THAT ALWAYS MAKE YOU LAUGH

INITIAL
HERE

--- ☐
--- ☐
--- ☐
--- ☐
--- ☐
--- ☐
--- ☐
--- ☐
--- ☐
--- ☐
--- ☐
--- ☐
--- ☐
--- ☐
--- ☐
--- ☐
--- ☐
--- ☐
--- ☐

SUNDAY NEWS

HOME

NEW YORK'S PICTURE NEWSPAPER

New York 17, Sunday, April 6, 2009   36 Main + 16 Comic

Vol. 26.   No. 49

GIRL CHOKES ON HER OWN SALIVA

Story on Page 15

LIST WHAT NEWSPAPER HEADLINE YOU'D GIVE YOUR CLOSEST ENCOUNTER WITH DEATH

INITIAL HERE

5 YEARS OLD: THE ROCKING CHAIR GHOST

LIST THE TIMES YOU'VE BEEN THE MOST SCARED

INITIAL
HERE

- --
- --
- --
- --
- --
- --
- --
- --
- --
- --
- --
- --
- --
- --
- --
- --
- --
- --
- --
- --

"OFFICE SPACE"

LIST THREE FAVORITE FILM COMEDIES

①   ②   ③   INITIAL HERE

NO-KILL ANIMAL SHELTERS

LIST THREE CAUSES YOU'D GIVE TIME OR MONEY TO

①   ②   ③   INITIAL HERE

A ROBOT

LIST THREE THINGS YOU'VE BEEN FOR HALLOWEEN

①   ②   ③   INITIAL HERE

"THE SHINING"

LIST YOUR THREE FAVORITE HORROR FILMS

①   ②   ③   INITIAL HERE

"I'M WITH THE BAND"

LIST WHAT YOUR AUTOBIOGRAPHY WOULD BE TITLED

INITIAL
HERE

THE GOLDEN LOTUS VEGETARIAN RESTAURANT

LIST YOUR THREE FAVORITE RESTAURANTS

①   ②   ③   INITIAL
HERE

VISIT ANTARCTICA

LIST THE THINGS YOU HAVE TO DO
BEFORE YOU DIE

INITIAL
HERE

-- ☐

-- ☐

-- ☐

-- ☐

-- ☐

-- ☐

-- ☐

-- ☐

-- ☐

-- ☐

-- ☐

-- ☐

-- ☐

-- ☐

-- ☐

-- ☐

-- ☐

-- ☐

"MAD MEN"

LIST YOUR TOP THREE FAVORITE
TV SHOWS OF ALL TIME

①   ②   ③   INITIAL HERE

MOSQUITOES IN THE HOUSE

LIST THREE THINGS THAT DRIVE YOU NUTS

①   ②   ③

INITIAL HERE

VILLAGE CHESS SHOP

LIST THREE OF YOUR FAVORITE PLACES TO SHOP

①   ②   ③   INITIAL HERE

LOLCATS WEB SITES

LIST THREE GUILTY PLEASURE WEB SITES

①   ②   ③   INITIAL HERE

"NOTES FROM THE UNDERGROUND"

LIST YOUR THREE FAVORITE BOOKS OF ALL TIME

①   ②   ③   INITIAL HERE

MY BEST FRIEND IN FIRST GRADE

LIST THREE THINGS YOU'VE LOST THAT YOU WANT TO GET BACK

①   ②   ③   INITIAL HERE

Michael Johnston

Katie Wood

Betty Minnow

Savitha Subram

Eddie Harold

Chad Goodie

REMEMBERING NAMES

LIST THREE THINGS YOU ARE INCREDIBLY BAD AT

①   ②   ③   INITIAL HERE

MR. STOCKTON

LIST TEACHERS YOU HAD A CRUSH ON

INITIAL
HERE

THE SOUND OF A POLAROID
CAMERA AND CAB HORNS

LIST SOUNDS YOU LOVE AND SOUNDS YOU HATE

LOVE   HATE   INITIAL
                                                                          HERE

CREATE YOUR OWN LIST

INITIAL
HERE

-- ☐
-- ☐
-- ☐
-- ☐
-- ☐
-- ☐
-- ☐
-- ☐
-- ☐
-- ☐
-- ☐
-- ☐
-- ☐
-- ☐
-- ☐
-- ☐
-- ☐
-- ☐
-- ☐

CREATE YOUR OWN LIST

INITIAL
HERE

- ☐

- ☐

- ☐

- ☐

- ☐

- ☐

- ☐

- ☐

- ☐

- ☐

- ☐

- ☐

- ☐

- ☐

- ☐

- ☐

- ☐

- ☐

- ☐

CREATE YOUR OWN LIST

INITIAL
HERE